A MILLENNIUM GUIDE TO THE CHRISTIAN SIGHTS

HOLY ROME

FODOR'S TRAVEL PUBLICATIONS, INC.
NEW YORK • TORONTO • LONDON • SYDNEY • AUCKLAND

WWW.FODORS.COM

CLEMENS XI
PONT·MAX·
FONTIS ET FORI
ORNAMENTO
ANNO SAL·
MDCCXI
PONTIF·XI